DiscoverRoo

An Imprint of Pop!
popbooksonline.com

Pop Biographies

OLIVIA RODRIGO

BEST-SELLING SONGWRITER

by Elizabeth Andrews

WELCOME TO
DiscoverRoo!

This book is filled with videos, puzzles, games, and more! Scan the QR codes* while you read, or visit the website below to make this book pop.

popbooksonline.com/rodrigo

abdobooks.com

Published by Pop!, a division of ABDO, PO Box 398166, Minneapolis, Minnesota 55439. Copyright © 2024 by Abdo Consulting Group, Inc. International copyrights reserved in all countries. No part of this book may be reproduced in any form without written permission from the publisher. DiscoverRoo™ is a trademark and logo of Pop!.

Printed in the United States of America, North Mankato, Minnesota.

052023
082023

THIS BOOK CONTAINS
RECYCLED MATERIALS

Cover Photo: Getty Images
Interior Photos: Getty Images, Shutterstock Images, Walt Disney Pictures/Kobal/Shutterstock, Chelsea Lauren/Shutterstock, Susan Walsh/AP/Shutterstock
Editor: Grace Hansen
Series Designer: Colleen McLaren

Library of Congress Control Number: 2022950566

Publisher's Cataloging-in-Publication Data

Names: Andrews, Elizabeth, author.
Title: Olivia Rodrigo: best-selling songwriter / by Elizabeth Andrews
Other title: best-selling songwriter
Description: Minneapolis, Minnesota : Pop!, 2024 | Series: Pop biographies | Includes online resources and index
Identifiers: ISBN 9781098244385 (lib. bdg.) | ISBN 9781098245085 (ebook)
Subjects: LCSH: Rodrigo, Olivia--Juvenile literature. | Singers--Juvenile literature. | Songwriters--Juvenile literature. | Actresses--Juvenile literature. | Disney Channel (Firm)--Juvenile literature.
Classification: DDC 782.42166092--dc23

*Scanning QR codes requires a web-enabled smart device with a QR code reader app and a camera.

TABLE OF
CONTENTS

CHAPTER 1

ALL OF THE TALENT

Olivia Isabel Rodrigo was born on February 20, 2003. She grew up in Temecula, California, with her mom and dad. Her mom was a schoolteacher, and her dad was a family **therapist**. Olivia and her family follow many traditions from her father's Filipino background.

WATCH A VIDEO HERE!

Olivia took piano lessons as a child.

Olivia started taking acting and vocal lessons when she was in kindergarten. As a kid, Olivia competed in local talent competitions and performed in school plays and musicals.

Olivia shared the Bizaardvark *screen with Madison Hu.*

Olivia's first acting role was in an Old
Navy advertisement. In 2015, she landed
a lead role in the American Girl film *Grace
Stirs Up Success*. Olivia was only 12!

Later that year she was cast in *Bizaardvark* for Disney Channel. It premiered in 2016. Olivia loved working with her co-star Madison Hu. The two girls played best friends who wrote songs and made music videos. The show aired for three seasons through 2019. These few roles were just the beginning for Olivia.

Olivia and Madison are good friends off screen too!

CHAPTER 2

HIGH SCHOOL MUSICAL MOMENT

Olivia attended elementary and middle school. She started homeschooling once she became a Disney star. After *Bizaardvark* ended, Disney gave Olivia her biggest role yet. She would play Nini in *High School Musical: The Musical: The Series* (*HSM:TM:TS*).

LEARN MORE HERE!

The series follows drama club members as they prepare for school performances. Olivia and her castmates sang and played instruments. This helped Olivia expand her musical talents.

Olivia's character Nini wrote songs in her bedroom. Olivia does the same thing in real life.

HIGH SCHOOL MUSICAL

The original High School Musical premiered in 2006.

HSM:TM:TS was a hit! Fans loved the **relatable** story lines. It was easy to see that the characters on the show had a bond in real life. It was a happy set to be on. Olivia and he co-star Joshua Bassett challenged each other to write one song a day during COVID-19 **quarantine**.

PRESS PAUSE

Filming *HSM:TM:TS* season 2 had to pause for six months when the COVID-19 **pandemic** hit. The same thing happened for many other shows and movies. Hollywood made changes to the way projects were filmed to keep actors and crew members safe and healthy.

DID YOU KNOW?

Olivia worried about what other people thought of her when she was 14. But she learned being true to herself was most important.

Olivia's character Nini could play the piano too!

Olivia wrote "All I Want" for her character Nini to perform. It was a hit. It sold more than 500,000 copies and became a gold record! The song was the first time Olivia felt like she directly connected with her fans.

The next year she and Joshua wrote and sang "Just for a Moment" on *HSM:TM:TS*. Olivia starred in the show for three seasons. Her character's exit from the show went hand in hand with the next chapter of Olivia's music journey.

In HSM:TM:TS Olivia also had to learn dance routines.

CHAPTER 3

SUPER SOUR

In January 2021, Olivia released her first **single** "drivers license." The single was not attached to her Disney career in any way. It was all her own, and it was a huge hit! The song started at #1 on the Billboard Hot 100.

EXPLORE LINKS HERE!

"drivers license" is a power ballad. Power ballads are slow rock songs with deep emotional lyrics sung strongly.

After "drivers license" was released, Olivia was invited to perform at all kinds of events.

Olivia's first single changed her life. She went from being an actor who sings to a vocal artist and songwriter. Olivia said she was very inspired by other songwriters like Taylor Swift and Jack White.

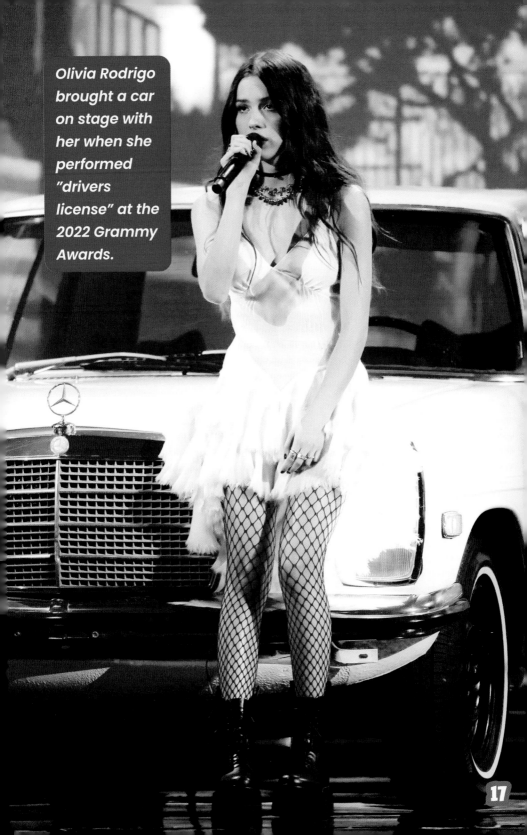

Olivia Rodrigo brought a car on stage with her when she performed "drivers license" at the 2022 Grammy Awards.

It seemed like "drivers license" had taken over the world. The song was everywhere from radio stations to Tik Tok. In March 2021, Olivia released her second single, "deja vu." The popular singles were the first introduction the world had to Olivia's debut album, *SOUR*. The album would feature songs that blended pop, folk, and alternative rock.

DID YOU KNOW?

"deja vu" debuted at #8 on the Billboard Top 100. Olivia Rodrigo became the first singer to have two debut singles in the top 10.

Olivia Rodrigo is friends with many other musicians including Lil Nas X.

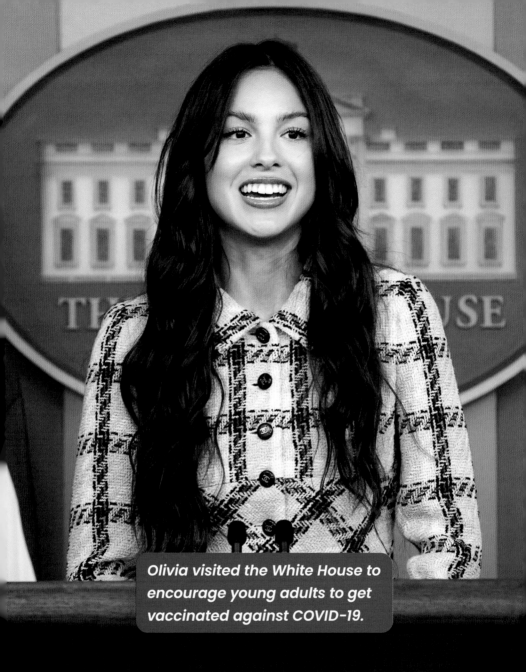

Olivia visited the White House to encourage young adults to get vaccinated against COVID-19.

THE WHITE HOUSE
WASHINGTON

SOUR was released on May 21, 2021. It was written by Olivia and her **producer** Dan Nigro. The album was supposed to be an **EP**, but its singles were so popular that they decided to expand it.

SOUR was listed as one of the best albums of 2021 by many **publications**. Its songs discussed themes of growing up, heartbreak, and friendship. Olivia's fans felt like they could see themselves in her music.

CHAPTER 4

TIME TO SHINE

Reviews for *SOUR* were very positive! Olivia was called one of the best songwriters and musicians of her **generation**. It's a meaningful claim because Olivia identifies first as a songwriter before her other talents and roles. It is her passion.

COMPLETE AN ACTIVITY HERE!

Olivia won six Moonmen at the 2021 MTV Video Music Awards.

GIRL'S GOT GRAMMYS

Best Pop Solo Performance

Best Pop Vocal Album

Best New Artist

Olivia really enjoys that her songs and lyrics take on a new life once she releases them. "Other people's stories get entwined with them," she said. The songs are no longer just hers. They belong to the world too.

Famous designers choose to dress Olivia for award shows. She wore Vivienne Westwood for the 2022 Grammys.

In April 2022, Olivia went on a North

American and European tour for *SOUR*.

On the road she performed with many

famous and meaningful artists. They

included Billy Joel, Lily Allen, Avril Lavigne,

Olivia Rodrigo performed with Billy Joel in August, 2022.

and Alanis Morissette. These were

musicians that Olivia looked up to!

Olivia Rodrigo makes music with her producer Dan Nigro.

Olivia isn't only busy with her music.

She uses her large fan base for good. In

July 2021 she visited the White House to

meet President Joe Biden. There, she spoke to encourage kids to get vaccinated against COVID-19. Olivia also brings attention to mental health and women's rights.

Olivia's next album was already in the works by 2023. She took her time and stayed close to her roots by writing songs in her bedroom. Olivia's stardom is just beginning!

Olivia wore butterflies in her hair at the 2022 MET Gala.

MAKING CONNECTIONS

TEXT-TO-SELF

Of all the roles, including songwriter, Olivia Rodrigo has had, which is your favorite? Please explain your answer.

TEXT-TO-TEXT

Have you read any other books about a singer who also acts? If so, how were they similar to and different from Olivia Rodrigo?

TEXT-TO-WORLD

Olivia Rodrigo visited the White House to help spread information about vaccines to young adults. Do you think it's important that people her age use their voices and fame to help the world be better?

GLOSSARY

EP — short for extended play album, a musical recording that contains more tracks than a single but fewer than a full album.

generation — the period of time between the birth of parents and the birth of their children.

pandemic — a disease outbreak that spreads to many countries.

producer — the person or company that makes something. Music producers put songs together.

publication — a magazine, book, newspaper, or other thing that is published.

quarantine — the keeping of a person, animal, or thing away from others to stop a disease from spreading.

relatable — enabling a person to feel that they can relate to or connect with someone or something.

single — a song that is released as a stand-alone from an album.

therapist — a person who specializes in helping people with emotional illnesses.

INDEX

**DiscoverRoo!
ONLINE RESOURCES**

This book is filled with videos, puzzles, games, and more! Scan the QR codes* while you read, or visit the website below to make this book pop.

popbooksonline.com/rodrigo

*Scanning QR codes requires a web-enabled smart device with a QR code reader app and a camera.